WORKING TOWARDS
EQUALITY

What Is SEXISM?

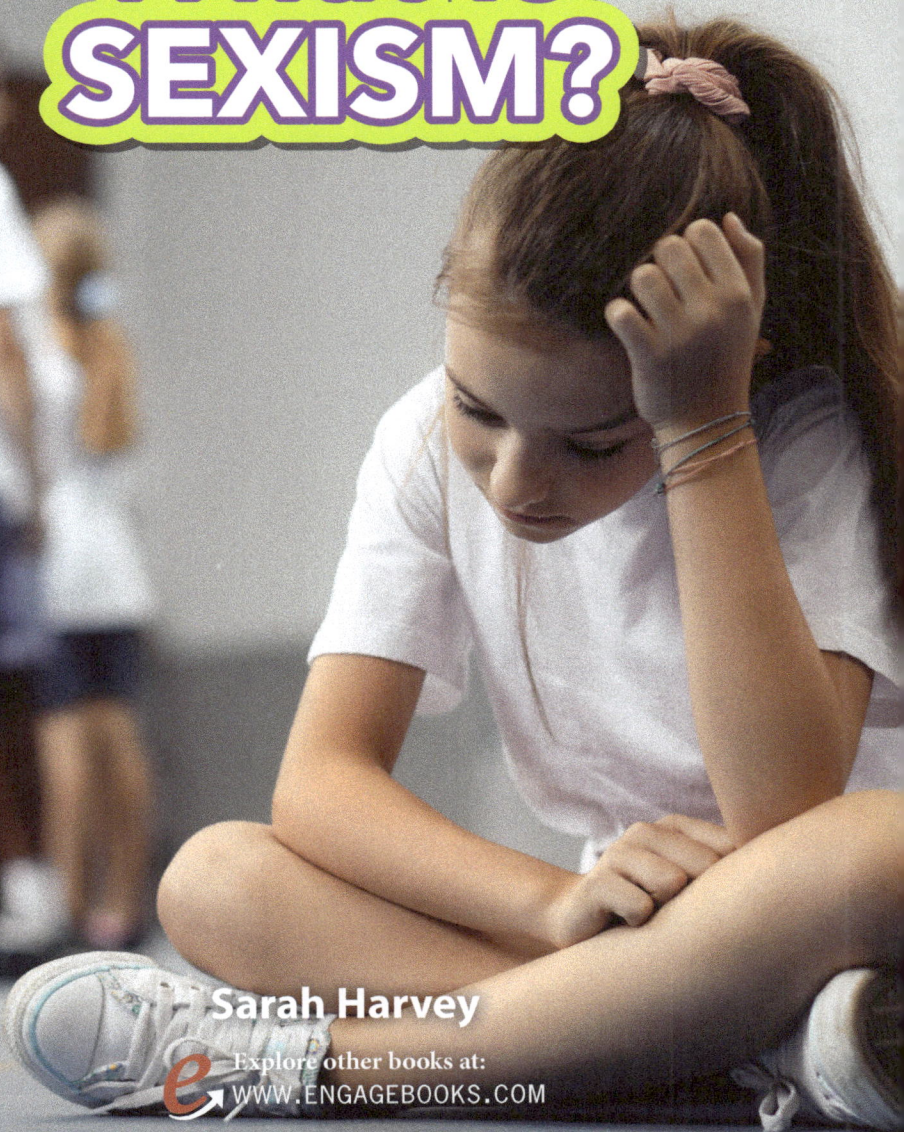

Sarah Harvey

Explore other books at:
WWW.ENGAGEBOOKS.COM

VANCOUVER, B.C.

e WWW.ENGAGEBOOKS.COM

What Is Sexism? - Working Towards Equality: Level 3
Harvey, Sarah 1950 –
Text © 2023 Engage Books
Design © 2023 Engage Books

Edited by: A.R. Roumanis and Ashley Lee
Design by: Mandy Christiansen

Text set in Montserrat Regular.
Chapter headings set in Merlo Neue.

FIRST EDITION / FIRST PRINTING

LIBRARY AND ARCHIVES CANADA CATALOGUING IN PUBLICATION

Title: What is sexism? / Sarah Harvey.
Names: Harvey, Sarah N., 1950- author.
Description: Series statement: Working towards equality

Identifiers: Canadiana (print) 20230447546 | Canadiana (ebook) 20230447554
ISBN 978-1-77476-851-8 (hardcover)
ISBN 978-1-77476-852-5 (softcover)
ISBN 978-1-77476-853-2 (epub)
ISBN 978-1-77476-854-9 (pdf)
ISBN 978-1-77878-132-2 (audio)

Subjects:
LCSH: Sexism—Juvenile literature.

Classification: LCC HQ1237 .H37 2023 | DDC J305.3—DC23

This project has been made possible in part
by the Government of Canada. | Canada

Contents

What Is Sexism?

Sexism is the belief that some people are not as good as others because of their sex or **gender identity**. Sex is a label a doctor gives a person depending on the body parts they have. A person's sex is either male or female.

KEY WORD

Gender identity: a person's inner sense of whether they are male, female, or something else.

More females than males experience sexism. Women often have to fight to be given the same rights as men. Girls may not be allowed to go to school in some countries.

Women are often paid less than men for the same work. This is called the gender pay gap.

What Is the Double Standard?

Traits are things that make someone unique. Gender **stereotypes** are traits that some people expect males or females to have. Some people judge males and females differently for the same traits. This is called the double standard.

KEY WORD

Stereotypes: common and basic thoughts about a group of people.

When boys stand up for themselves and take charge, they are called leaders. If girls act this way, they are often called bossy. Boys may be made fun of if they show their emotions, but girls are not.

People may hide their thoughts or feelings if they know they will be judged for them.

Kinds of Sexism

Hostile sexism is when someone is **aggressive** towards another sex or gender identity. They often think other sexes or gender identities are bad. This is common when men think they should be in charge of women.

KEY WORD

Aggressive: behaviors such as yelling or violence that can scare or hurt another person.

Benevolent Sexism is not aggressive. It can happen when a man thinks a woman needs to be protected. They think women are not as strong as men and believe in gender stereotypes.

Ambivalent sexism is when someone becomes angry when others do not follow common gender stereotypes. They do not think other sexes or gender identities are bad.

The History of Sexism 1

In the early 1800s, women were not allowed to **vote** or own a home. They began to work together to demand equal rights. This was called women's suffrage. In 1893, New Zealand became the first country to allow women to vote.

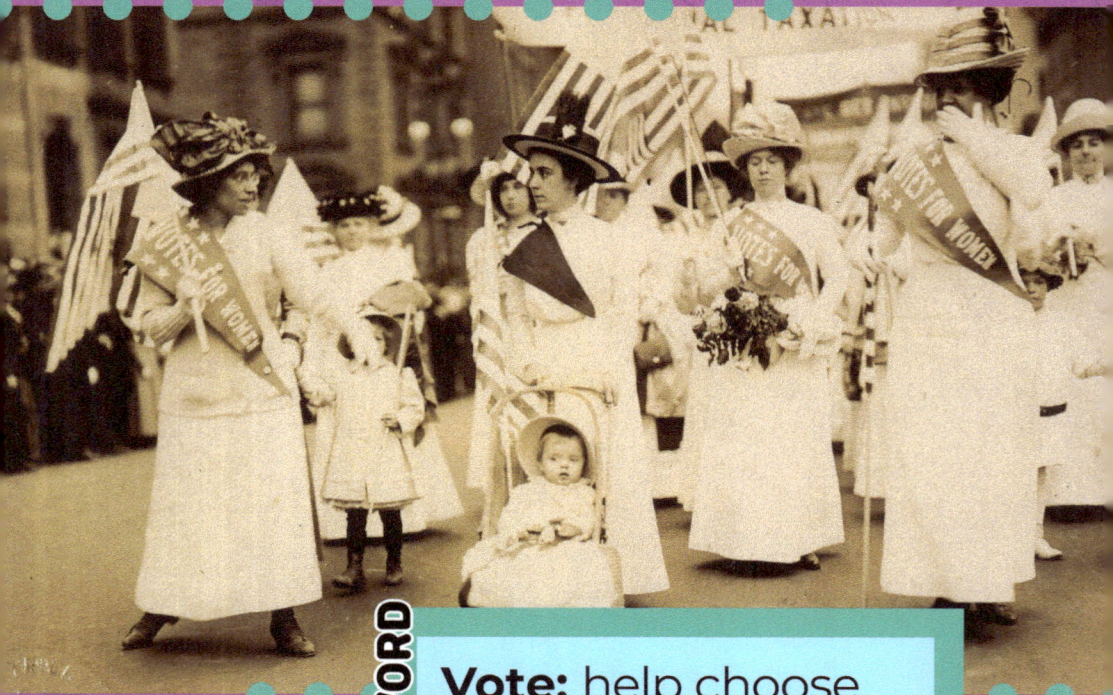

KEY WORD

Vote: help choose government leaders.

Oberlin College opened in 1833. It was the first **college or university** to allow men and women to learn together. Many other colleges and universities did not allow this until the 1960s and 1970s. They did not want women in their schools.

11

History of Sexism 2

Until the 1900s, women mostly worked in offices, shops or schools. When World War II started in 1939, many men were forced to become soldiers. Women had to take over men's jobs in **factories**.

KEY WORD

Factories: places where machines are used to make things people can buy.

For a long time, women were not allowed to play as many sports as men. Men thought sports were too manly and women would hurt themselves. In 1967, Katherine Switzer became the first woman to run in the Boston **Marathon**.

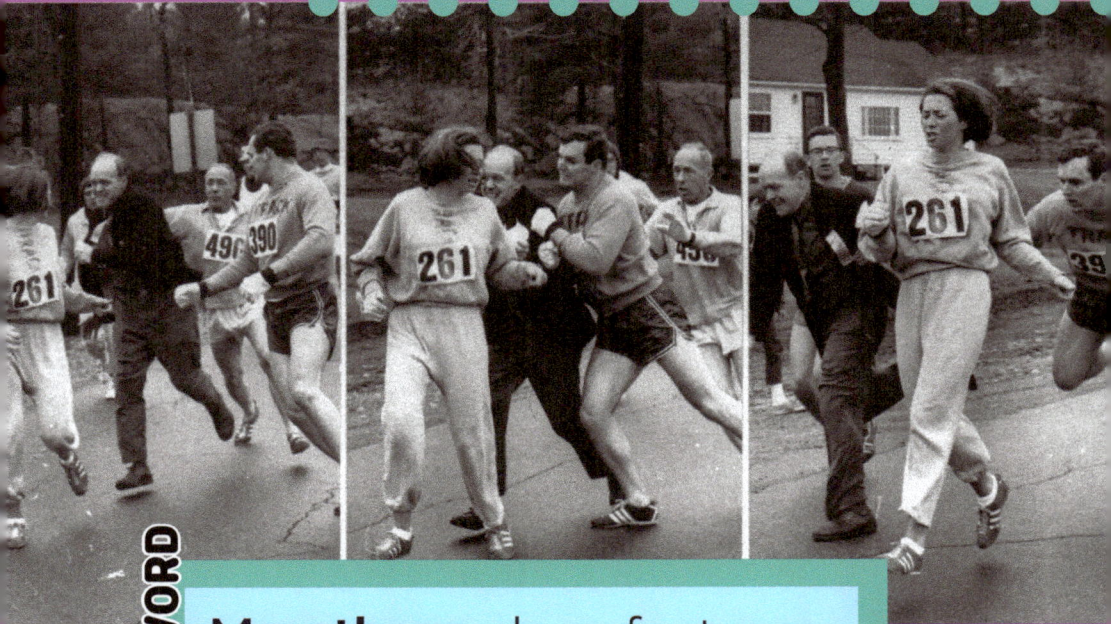

KEY WORD

Marathon: a long foot race.

Why Are People Sexist?

Sexism is a learned behavior. Children see and hear adults and **peers** being sexist. People may try to fit in with others by saying or doing sexist things.

Children as young as three or four can be sexist.

Movies and TV shows often show sexist behaviors. These behaviors can also be seen all over social media. This can make it seem as though these behaviors are normal or okay.

What Does Sexism Look Like?

Sexism is shown through words, actions, and images. Jokes that put women and girls down are sexist. Telling a boy he "throws like a girl" is sexist. Sexism can happen at home, at school, or at someone's place of work.

At home, girls might be expected to do pink jobs. These are things like washing dishes or doing laundry. Boys might be asked to do blue jobs. These are jobs that are thought to be dirty or rough, like mowing the lawn or washing the car.

What to Do if You Experience Sexism 1

If you feel comfortable talking to the person, ask them if they know they are being sexist. Some people may not know. This can be a good chance to teach them about sexism.

Tell a trusted adult if you feel uncomfortable or unsafe with someone's sexist behavior. This behavior is not okay. You do not have to put up with it.

What to Do if You Experience Sexism 2

You might see someone being sexist towards a friend. Ask your friend if they need help before helping them. They may want to deal with the problem on their own.

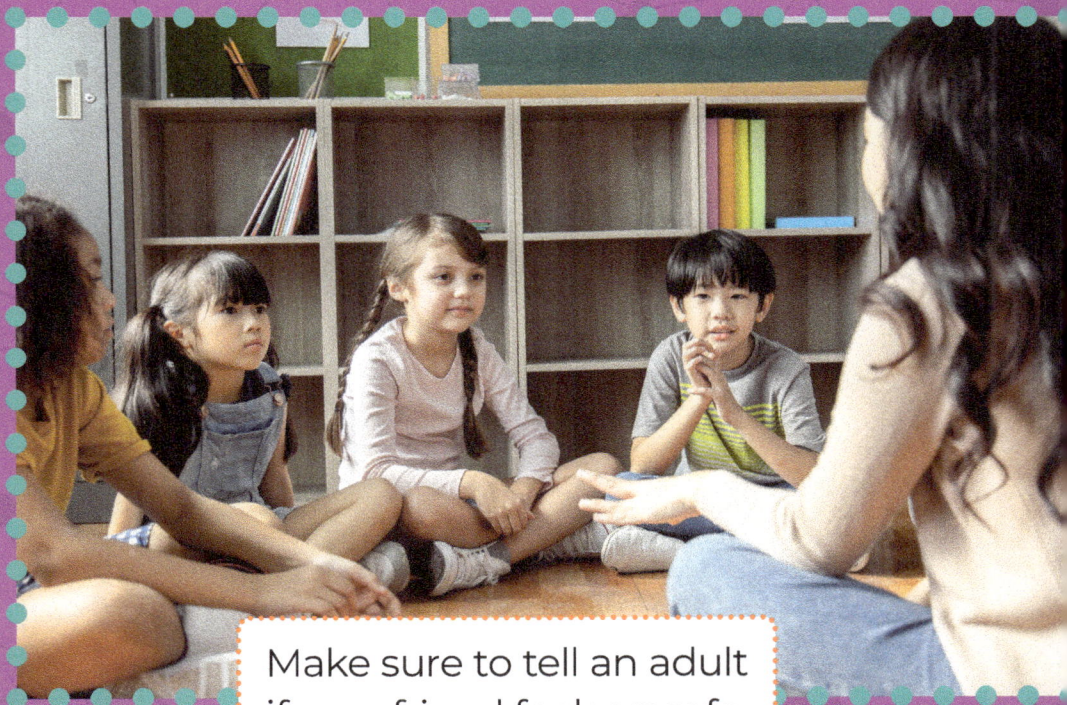

Make sure to tell an adult if your friend feels unsafe.

If your friend does want help, you can try to get them away from the person being sexist. Try to support them. They may want to talk to you about their experience or they may not.

Equality Superheroes in the Past

Elizabeth Cady Stanton and **Lucretia Mott** organized the first women's rights event in 1848 in New York State. They believed in a woman's right to own property, to vote, and to be paid the same as a man.

"The best protection any woman can have ... is courage."
—Elizabeth Cady Stanton

Susan B. Anthony met Elizabeth Cady Stanton in 1851. Together they founded the American Equal Rights Association. She died 14 years before American women won the right to vote.

"Failure is impossible."
—Susan B. Anthony

Sojourner Truth was born a slave in New York State in about 1797. She became an **abolitionist** and women's rights activist after she was freed from slavery. She worked for the rights of slaves and women until her death in 1883.

KEY WORD

Abolitionist: a person who works to end slavery.

"The truth is powerful and it prevails."
—Sojourner Truth

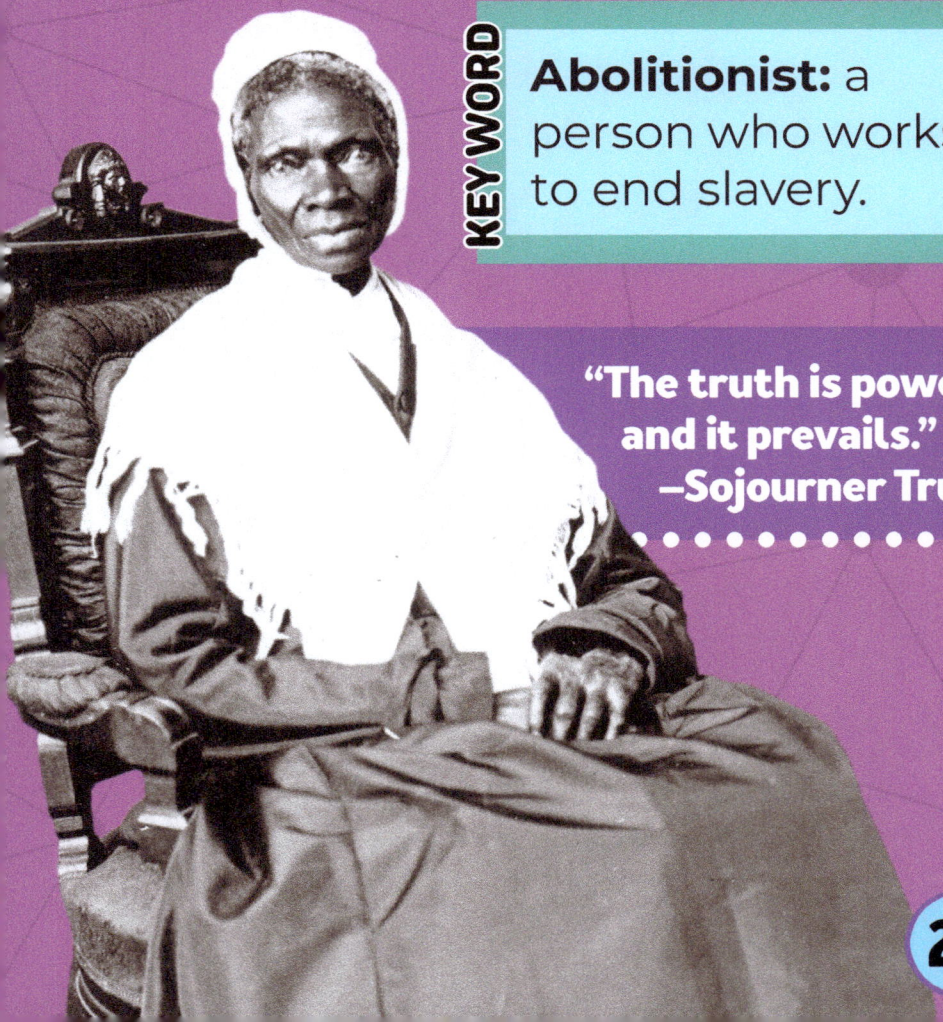

23

Equality Superheroes Today

Gloria Steinem is an American journalist and women's rights activist. In 1972, she cofounded the women's rights magazine called *Ms*. She has spent her life giving speeches and writing about women's issues. In 2017, she received the Presidential Medal of Freedom.

> "When unique voices are united in a common cause, they make history."
> —Gloria Steinem

Mark Ruffalo plays the Hulk in the Marvel movies. He speaks up when he sees female actors being paid less than male actors. He often voices support for a woman's right to do what she wants with her own body.

Michelle Obama was First Lady of the United States of America. In addition to being a wife, mother, and lawyer, she has helped other women succeed. Her project called Let Girls Learn has helped educate millions of girls worldwide.

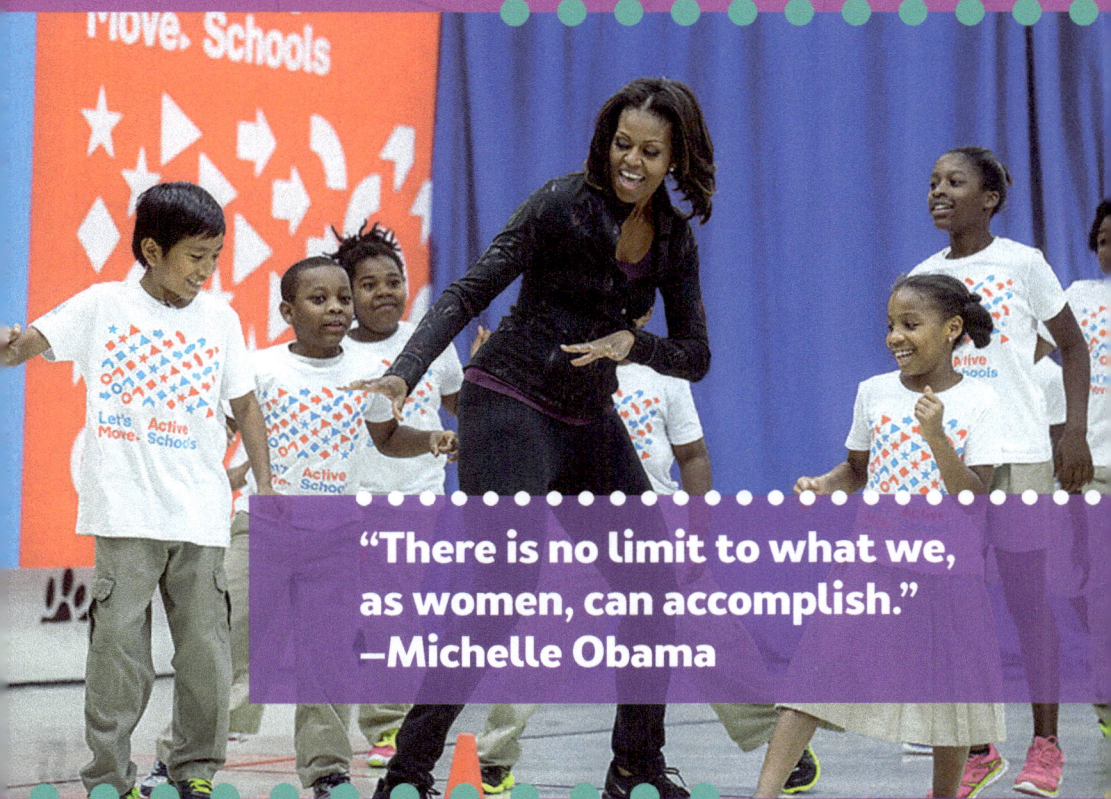

"There is no limit to what we, as women, can accomplish."
—Michelle Obama

Ways to Support Change 1

Sexist language leaves people out or makes fun of them. When you are speaking or writing, try to use **inclusive** language. Saying police officer instead of policeman is more inclusive.

KEY WORD

Inclusive: leaving no one out.

Ways to Support Change 2

Be aware of gender stereotypes movies, TV shows, or music. If you think a certain song or show is sexist, talk to your friends and family about it. Talking about sexism helps you understand how it works.

Ways to Support Change 3

If you see or hear something that seems unfair or wrong, ask yourself a question. Is the way a girl looks more important than how she treats others? Why can a boy not wear a dress if he wants to?
Your answers
will help you
treat all
people equally.

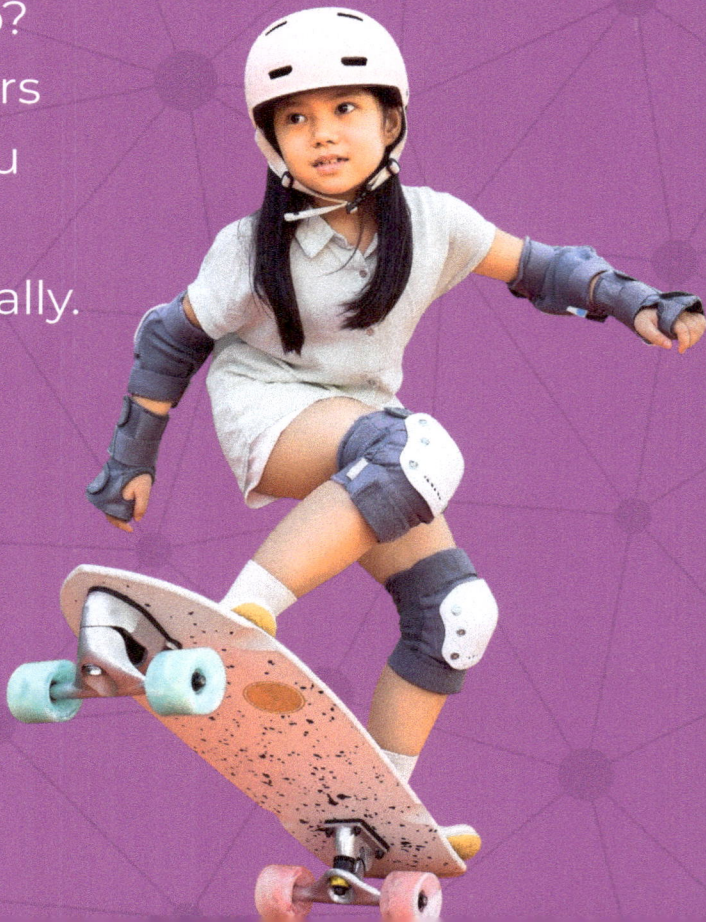

Speaking out against sexism can be hard, no matter how old you are.

Ways to Support Change 4

Many people want women to be treated the same as men. They often call themselves feminists. Call out sexism when you can. Show the world what equality means.

Quiz

Test your knowledge of sexism by answering the following questions. The questions are based on what you have read in this book. The answers are listed on the bottom of the next page.

1 What is gender identity?

2 What is hostile sexism?

3 What was the first country to allow women to vote?

4 Where can sexism happen?

5 What kind of language should you try to use when speaking or writing?

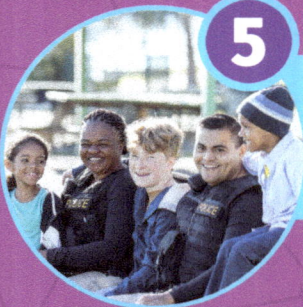

6 What award did Gloria Steinem receive in 2017?

Explore Other Level 3 Readers.

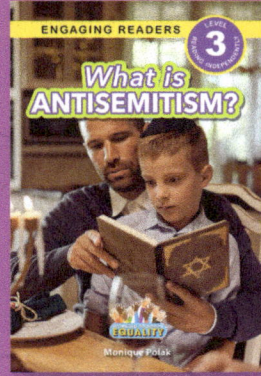

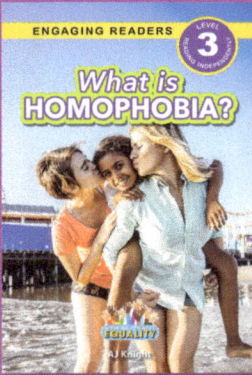

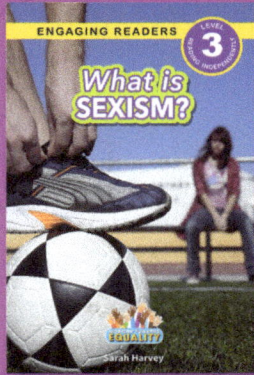

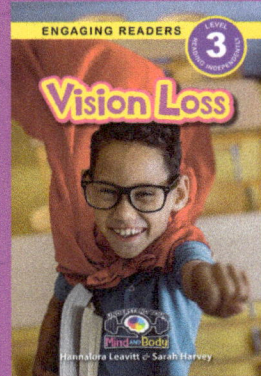

ENGAGING READERS — LEVEL 3
What is ABLEISM?
EQUALITY
Adelaide Wilder

ENGAGING READERS — LEVEL 3
What is AGEISM?
EQUALITY
Sarah Harvey

ENGAGING READERS — LEVEL 3
What is ANTISEMITISM?
EQUALITY
Monique Polak

ENGAGING READERS — LEVEL 3
What is HOMOPHOBIA?
EQUALITY
AJ Knight

ENGAGING READERS — LEVEL 3
What is SEXISM?
EQUALITY
Sarah Harvey

ENGAGING READERS — LEVEL 3
Diabetes
Mind and Body
Kit Caudron-Robinson

ENGAGING READERS — LEVEL 3
Obesity
Mind and Body
Kit Caudron-Robinson

ENGAGING READERS — LEVEL 3
Autism
Mind and Body
AJ Knight

ENGAGING READERS — LEVEL 3
Vision Loss
Mind and Body
Hannalora Leavitt & Sarah Harvey

Visit www.engagebooks.com/readers

Answers: 1. A person's inner sense of whether they are male, female, or something else 2. When someone is aggressive towards a another sex or gender identity 3. New Zealand 4. At home, at school, or at someone's place of work 5. Inclusive language 6. The Presidential Medal of Freedom

www.ingramcontent.com/pod-product-compliance
Lightning Source LLC
Chambersburg PA
CBHW051241020426
42331CB00016B/3478